Life Cycle of an

Oak Tree

Angela Royston

For more information about Heinemann Library books, or to order, please telephone +44 (0)1865 888066, or send a fax to +44 (0)1865 314091. You can visit our web site at www.heinemann.co.uk

First published in Great Britain by Heinemann Library,
Halley Court, Jordan Hill, Oxford OX2 8EJ
a division of Reed Educational and Professional Publishing Ltd.
Heinemann is a registered trademark of Reed Educational & Professional Publishing Ltd.

OXFORD   MELBOURNE   AUCKLAND
JOHANNESBURG   BLANTYRE   GABORONE
IBADAN   PORTSMOUTH (NH) USA   CHICAGO

Designed by Celia Floyd
Illustrations by Alan Fraser
Printed in China by South China Printing Co. Ltd.

05 04 03 02 01
10 9 8 7 6 5 4 3 2 1

ISBN 0 431 083967
This title is also available in a hardback library edition (ISBN 0 43108391 6)

British Library Cataloguing in Publication Data

Royston, Angela
  Life cycle of an oak tree
  1. Oak – Life cycles – Juvenile literature
  I. Title   II. Oak tree
  583.4'6

Acknowledgements
The Publisher would like to thank the following for permission to reproduce photographs:

Ardea London: p.8, p.11, Bob Gibbons p.27, JA Bailey p.19; Bruce Coleman Collection: Andrew Purcell p.12, Norbert Schwirtz p.20; NHPA: Brian Hawkes p.18, Daniel Heuclin p.6, p.7, Roger Tidman p.17, Stephen Dalton p.21, p.24; Oxford Scientific Films: Alastair Shay p.22, Chris Sharp p.25, Deni Bown p.15, Niall Benvie p.10, Tim Shepherd p.4; Planet Earth Pictures: Rosemary Calvert p.14; Wildlife Matters: p.5, p.9, p.16, p.23, p.26, Sheila Apps p.13.

Cover photograph reproduced with the permission of Bruce Coleman.

Every effort has been made to contact copyright holders of any material reproduced in this book. Any omissions will be rectified in subsequent printings if notice is given to the Publisher.

Contents

The mighty oak

There are thousands of different kinds of tree. You can tell them apart by the shape and colour of their leaves.

Acorn

Sapling

Catkins

Every oak tree grows from a **seed** called an acorn. This book tells the story of how a mighty oak tree grew from a single acorn.

4 months later   70 years   Hundreds of years

An acorn

The acorn has been lying in the ground in the forest all winter. In spring the sun warms up the soil and the acorn begins to grow.

Acorn

Sapling

Catkins

A **root** grows down through the soil
and a shoot pushes up into the air. The
roots take in water from the soil and
the leaves open.

4 months later

70 years

Hundreds of years

I year old

The young tree is called a **sapling**. The leaves use sunlight, air and water to make food for the tree.

Acorn

Sapling

Catkins

The food keeps the sapling alive and helps it grow bigger and stronger. It starts to grow more twigs and small **branches**.

4 months later   70 years   Hundreds of years

Autumn

In autumn the leaves change colour from green to red, yellow and brown. They slowly dry up, die and fall from the tree.

Acorn

Sapling

Catkins

New **buds** form on the tree, ready to grow into leaves and twigs next spring. The **sapling** and all the other trees in the forest rest through the cold winter.

 4 months later

70 years

 Hundreds of years

20 years old

12

Every year the tree produces new leaves and twigs and grows taller. The twigs become **branches** and the **trunk** grows thicker.

Acorn   Sapling   Catkins

Now spring is coming again and the new **buds** are beginning to open. The buds will open out into new leaves.

4 months later

70 years

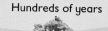

Hundreds of years

1 month later

The tree is covered in **catkins**. The long catkins are male. The wind blows the **pollen** from them onto the **female** flowers of another oak.

Acorn

Sapling

Catkins

The shorter catkins are female flowers. Some of the eggs in the female flower join with grains of pollen to make new **seeds**.

4 months later

70 years

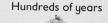
Hundreds of years

4 months later

The new **seeds** swell and grow. They are called acorns. In autumn, birds, squirrels and other animals love to eat ripe acorns!

Acorn

Sapling

Catkins

Squirrels sometimes bury acorns to eat later but forget where they are. Some buried acorns may grow into new **saplings** next spring.

4 months later

70 years

Hundreds of years

70 years old

The tree has now lived as long as some people. Its **trunk** is tall and strong, and many kinds of animals live in the tree.

Acorn

Sapling

Catkins

Several birds have built a nest among the leaves and twigs. Thousands of insects live in the **bark** and on the leaves.

4 months later   70 years   Hundreds of years

6 months later

A **gall wasp** has laid its eggs
under this leaf. The oak tree makes
a special growth around each egg.
The growth looks like an apple.

Acorn

Sapling

Catkins

The egg hatches into a grub. The grub eats the 'oak apple' instead of the leaves. Now the grub has changed into a new gall wasp.

4 months later

70 years

Hundreds of years

Many years later

A storm hits the forest. A mighty wind whips through the trees. **Branches** crack and some of the trees are blown over.

Acorn

Sapling

Catkins

The top of one tree breaks off and crashes to the ground! The rest of the tree is still alive, and will carry on growing.

4 months later   70 years   Hundreds of years

Fact file

There are 450 different kinds of oak tree. Most oak trees live for up to 400 years, but the English oak tree in this book could live for 900 years.

The **bark** of the cork oak is used to make corks for bottles, cork tiles and was once used inside life jackets to make them **float**.

Oak trees may have 400 different kinds of insects, spiders, worms, mice, birds and other animals living on them.

Some oak **galls** are used to make dyes which are used in making leather.

Glossary

bark   hard layer of wood that covers the trunk and branches of a tree

branches   the small twigs grow longer and thicker and become branches

buds   small swellings which will grow into new leaves or flowers

female   girl

float   does not sink

gall wasp   insect which lays eggs on oak trees

hollow   empty

male   boy

pollen   fine grains of powder produced by the male part of plants and trees

root   part of a plant or tree that takes in water and food from the ground

sapling   a tiny young tree

seed   male pollen joins with a female egg to become a seed which can grow into a new plant

trunk   the main, strong stem of a tree

Index